This Book Belongs
To

_____

OUR BOOK RANGE

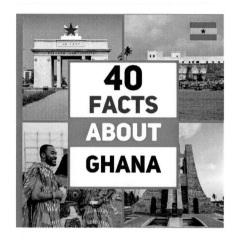

For more visit
www.grantpublishingltd.com

Book design and editing by Josephine Grant
Images from Canva

40 Facts About Ethiopia

Grant Publishing

40 Facts About Ethiopia

Let's learn something

Bite-sized facts and stunning photographs about the wonderful country that is Ethiopia. A great choice to introduce your child to the world around them.

GRANT
PUBLISHING

Ethiopia is a country in the continent of Africa.

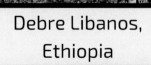

Debre Libanos, Ethiopia

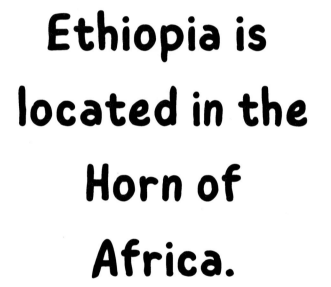

Ethiopia is located in the Horn of Africa.

Dancalia, Ethiopia

People from Ethiopia are called Ethiopian.

Lalibela, Ethiopia

Ethiopia is approximately 1,100,000 square kilometres.

Women carrying water in Ethiopia

Ethiopia is officially the Federal Democratic Republic of Ethiopia.

Bole, Addis Ababa, Ethiopia

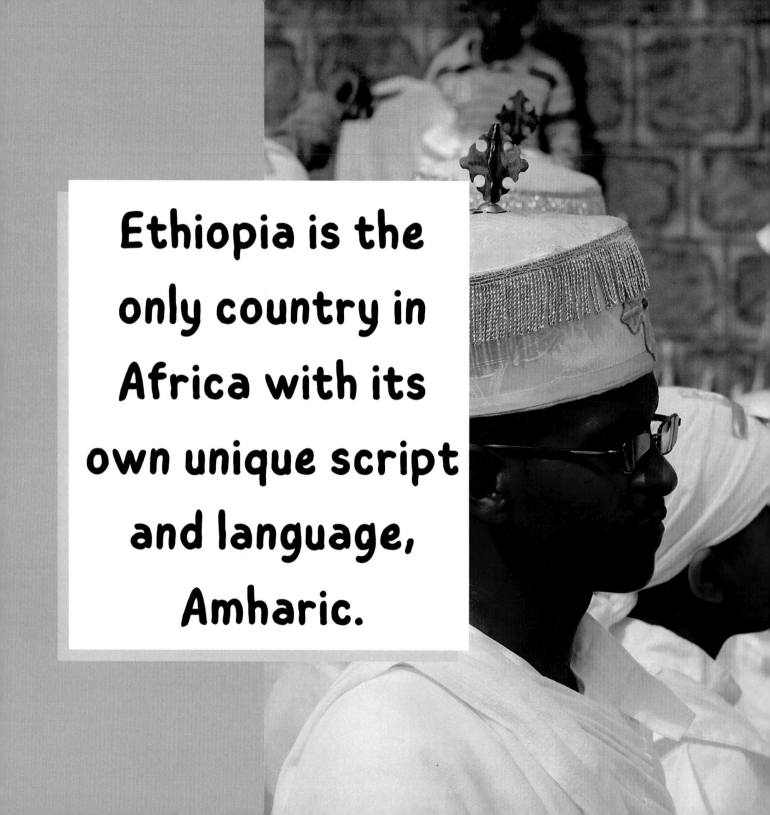

Ethiopia is the only country in Africa with its own unique script and language, Amharic.

Ethiopia is the largest producer of honey in Africa.

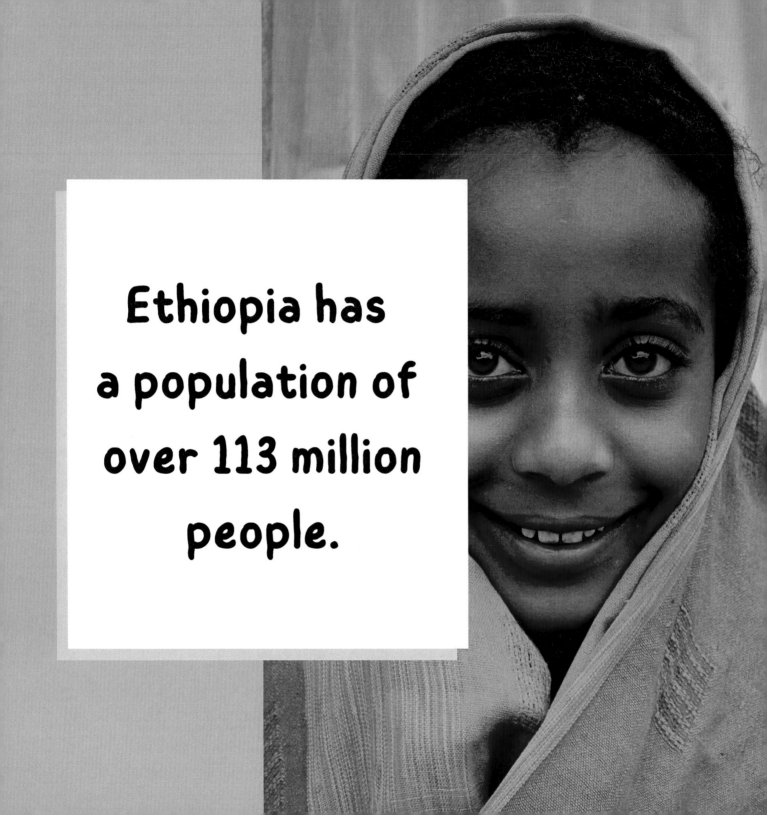

Ethiopia has
a population of
over 113 million
people.

Ethiopia is the 13th most populous country in the world.

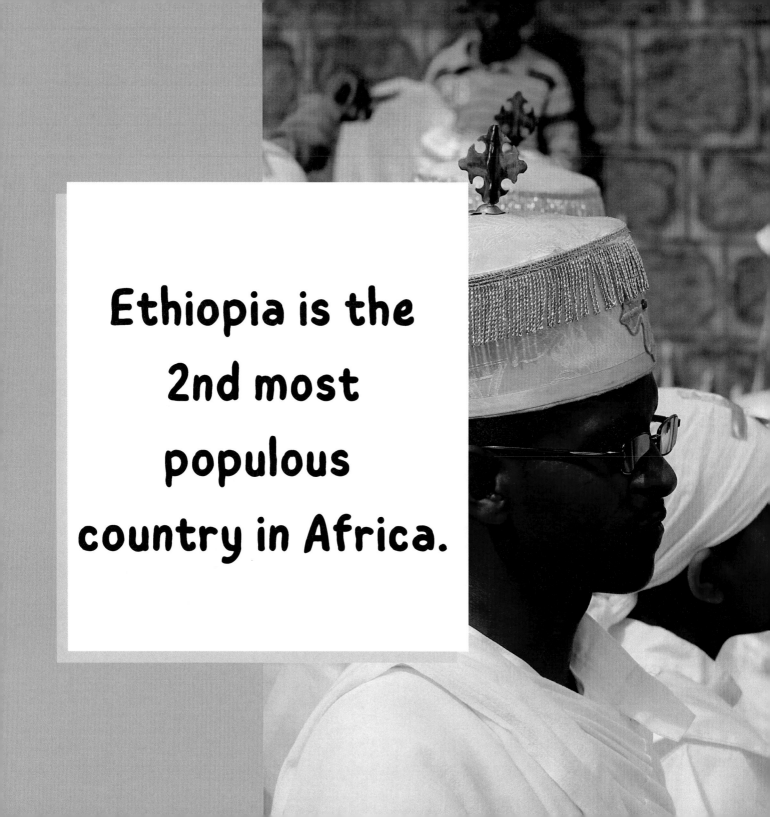

Ethiopia is the 2nd most populous country in Africa.

The capital city of Ethiopia is Addis Ababa.

Addis Ababa, Ethiopia

The famous coffee bean is believed to have originated in Ethiopia.

Traditional Coffee Ceremony in Ethiopia

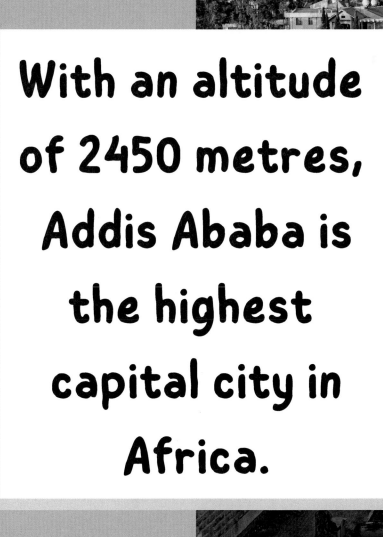

With an altitude of 2450 metres, Addis Ababa is the highest capital city in Africa.

Addis Ababa, Ethiopia

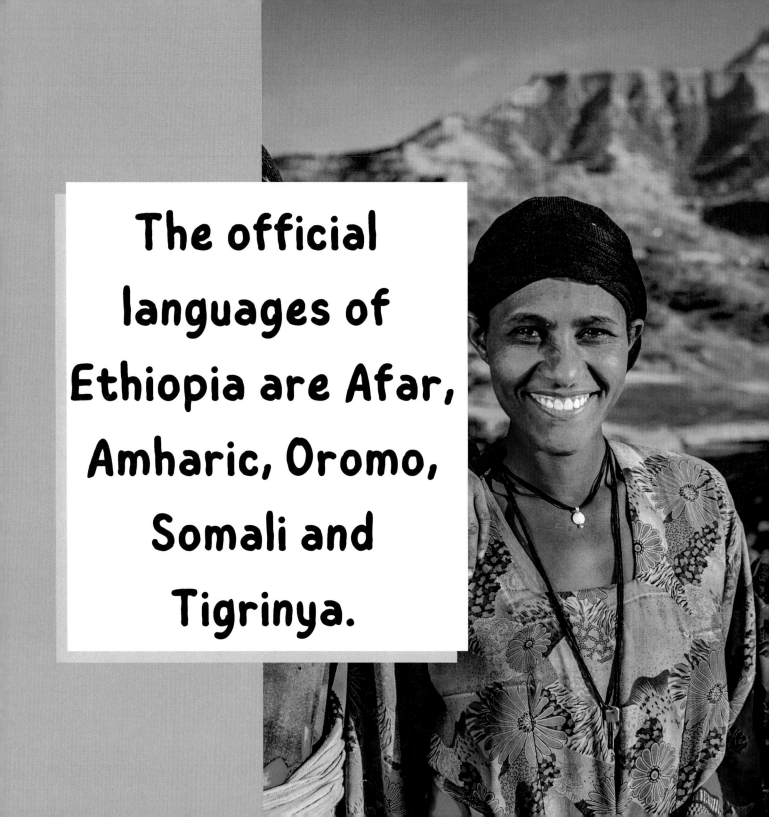

The official languages of Ethiopia are Afar, Amharic, Oromo, Somali and Tigrinya.

The regional languages of Ethiopia are Harari and Sidama.

Northern Ethiopia

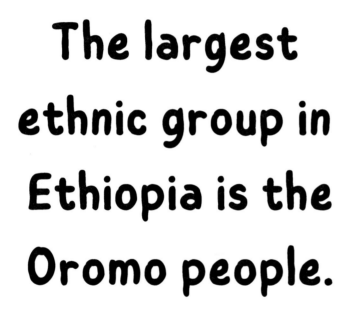

The largest ethnic group in Ethiopia is the Oromo people.

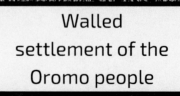

Walled settlement of the Oromo people

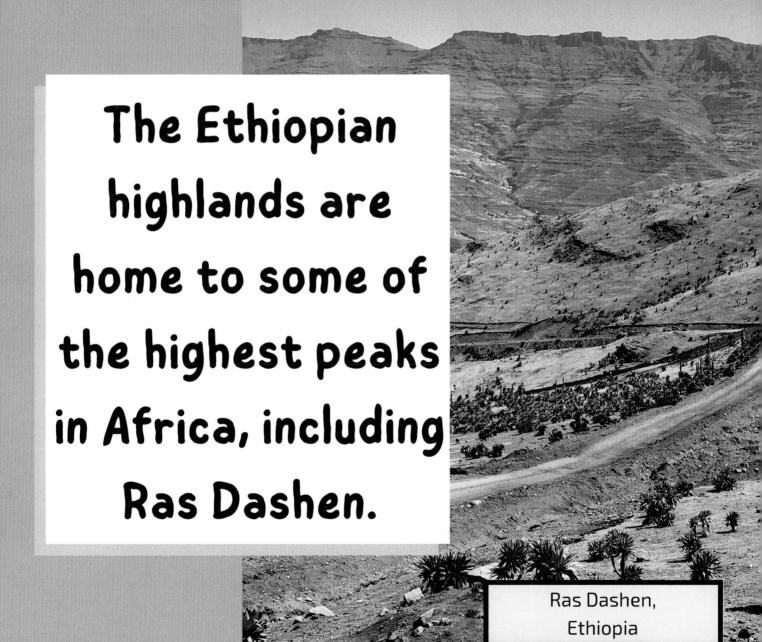

The Ethiopian highlands are home to some of the highest peaks in Africa, including Ras Dashen.

Ras Dashen, Ethiopia

The national anthem of Ethiopia is 'March Forward, Dear Mother Ethiopia'.

Ethiopia is the only African country to have never been brought under colonial control.

Kosoye, Ethiopia

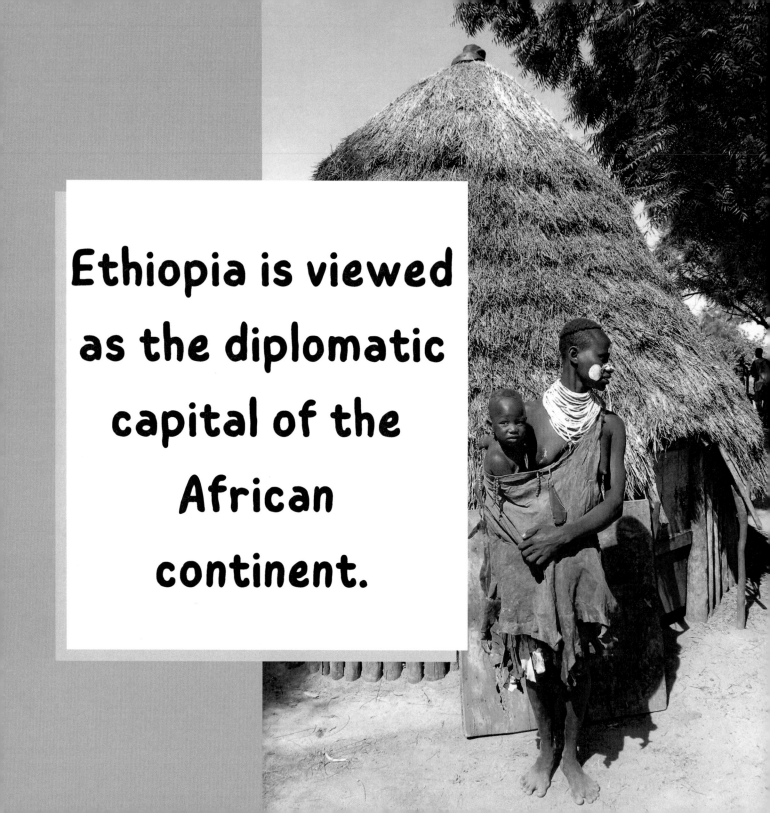

Ethiopia is viewed as the diplomatic capital of the African continent.

Ethiopia was the first African nation to join the League of Nations.

The largest religion in Ethiopia is Christianity.

Saint Mary's Tsion Church, Ethiopia

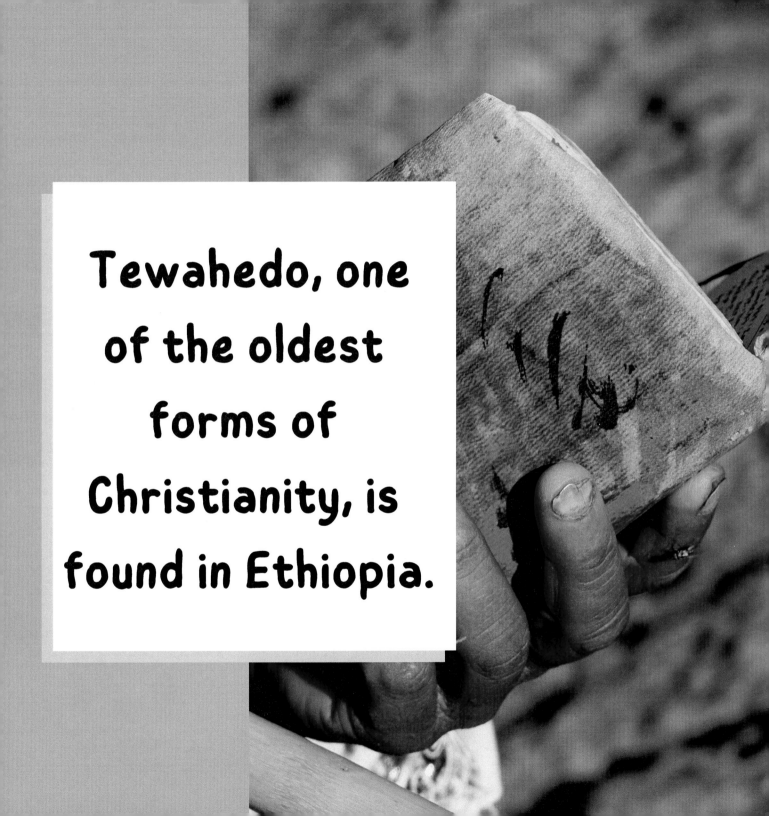

Tewahedo, one of the oldest forms of Christianity, is found in Ethiopia.

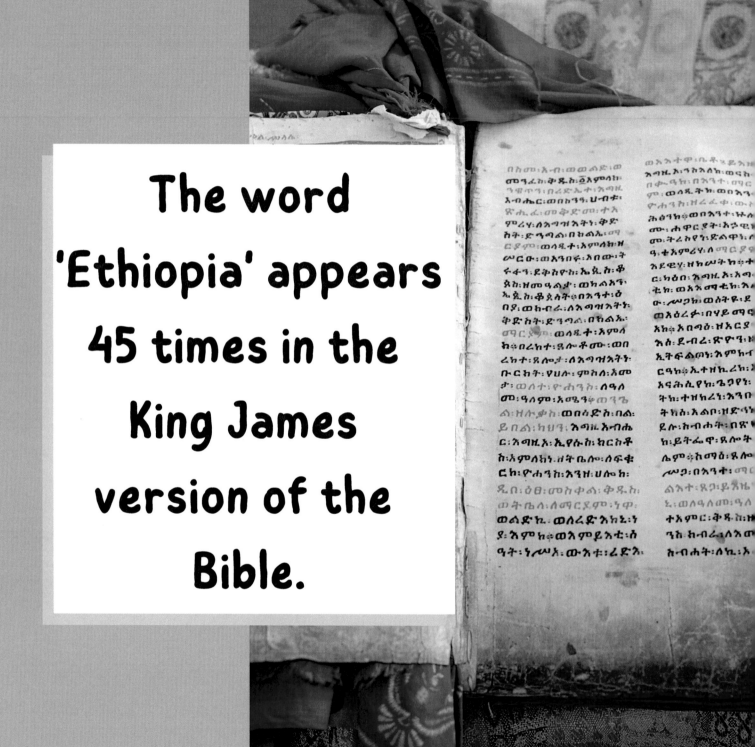

The word 'Ethiopia' appears 45 times in the King James version of the Bible.

Ethiopia was the first country in the world to accept Islam as a religion.

Mosque in Gondar, Ethiopia

Ethiopia is the birthplace of the Rastafarian movement.

Ethiopia is the
birthplace of
Pan-Africanism.

The Ethiopian Empire was established in 1270.

Ethiopia is home to nine UNESCO World Heritage Sites, including the ancient city of Aksum

Aksum obelisks, Ethiopia

Ethiopia has its own calendar that differs from the Gregorian Calendar.

The Ethiopian calendar has 13 months.

Macalle, Ethiopia

The national animal of Ethiopia is the Lion.

There are wide diversity of animals and birds found in Ethiopia.

Mammals found in Ethiopia include hippos, crocodiles, monkeys and elephants.

The currency
in Ethiopia is
the Birr.

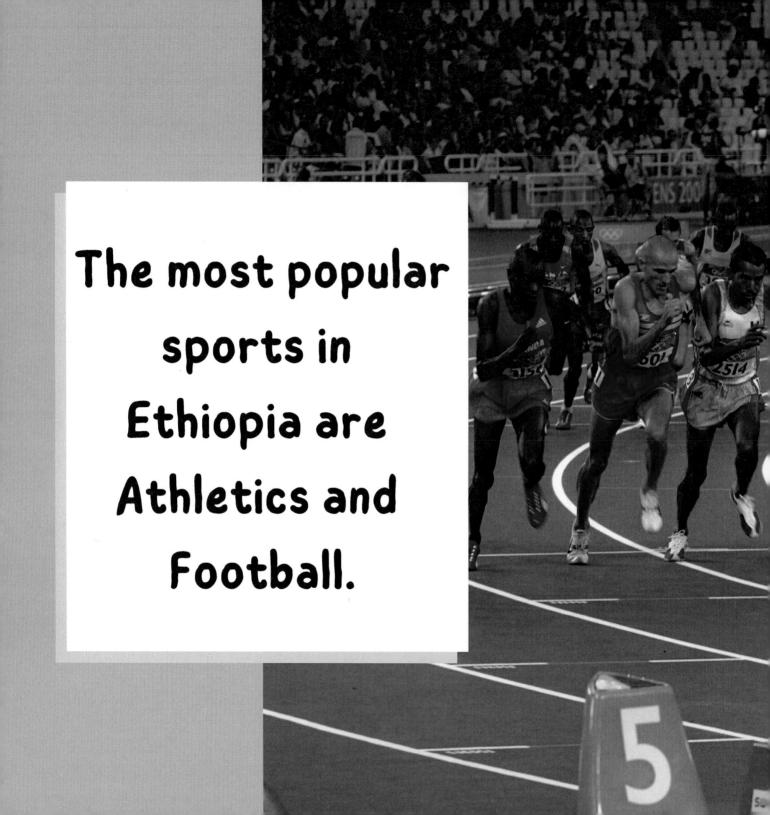

The most popular sports in Ethiopia are Athletics and Football.

The biggest festival in Ethiopia is called Timkat.

Timkat Cortege

Ethiopia has one of the lowest rates of motor vehicle ownership in the world.

Harar, Ethiopia

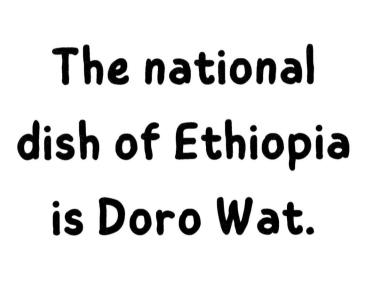

The national dish of Ethiopia is Doro Wat.

Doro Wat

The Great Rift Valley, which runs through Ethiopia, is an important site for studying human evolution.

WHAT WAS YOUR FAVOURITE FACT?

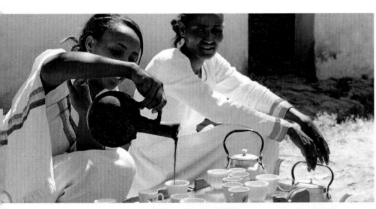

Made in United States
North Haven, CT
17 June 2023

37845474R00027